First Facts

Community Helpers at Work

A Day in the
Life of a
Police Officer

2981 3695

by Heather Adamson

Consultant:
Jeffrey B. Bumgarner, Ph.D.
Department of Political Science and Law Enforcement
Minnesota State University, Mankato

Capstone
press

Mankato, Minnesota

First Facts is published by Capstone Press
151 Good Counsel Drive, P.O. Box 669, Mankato, Minnesota 56002
http://www.capstone-press.com

Library of Congress Cataloging-in-Publication Data
Adamson, Heather, 1974—
  A day in the life of a police officer / by Heather Adamson.
  p. cm.— (First facts. Community helpers at work)
  Includes bibliographical references and index.
  Contents: What do police officers wear during their shifts?—What happens at a briefing?—What do police officers drive?—How do police officers know where help is needed?—How do police officers help in emergencies?—What do police officers do when they are not stopping crime?—How do police officers know if someone is speeding?—What happens at the end of a shift?
  ISBN 0-7368-2285-2 (hardcover)
  1. Police—Juvenile literature. 2. Police patrol—Juvenile literature. [1. Police. 2. Police patrol. 3. Occupations.] I. Title. II. Series.
HV7922.A33 2004
363.2—dc21   2003000152

Credits
Jennifer Schonborn, designer; Jim Foell, photographer; Eric Kudalis,
  product planning editor

Artistic Effects
Ingram Publishing, PhotoDisc

Capstone Press wishes to thank Officer David Queen and the Minneapolis Police
  Department for their help in the photographing of this book.

1 2 3 4 5 6 08 07 06 05 04 03

Table of Contents

What do police officers wear during their shifts?

Police officers wear uniforms with badges. Uniforms help people notice officers who are working. Officer David wears a bulletproof vest under his shirt. He carries handcuffs, a gun, and a baton on his belt. His belt also holds a two-way radio to contact the station.

Fun Fact:
More than 441,000 people work as city police officers in the United States.

6:00 in the
morning

7:00 in the morning

What happens at a briefing?

Officers meet with the sergeant for a briefing at the start of each shift. The sergeant explains any crimes that happened during the last shift. The sergeant also tells the officers their duties. Officer David and Officer Melissa will work together on patrol.

What do police officers drive?

Police officers use many kinds of vehicles to patrol. They sometimes use bikes or horses.

David drives a patrol car. The car has lights,
a siren, a radio, a camera, and a computer.
Officer David drives around watching for
crime. He looks for anyone who needs help.

How do police officers know where help is needed?

Dispatchers answer 911 phone calls and tell police officers where to go. While David and Melissa are eating lunch, the dispatcher's voice comes over the radio. It says, "10-52." This means there is a car crash with injuries. David and Melissa rush to the scene a few blocks away.

How do police officers help in emergencies?

Police officers are trained to work quickly in an emergency. David directs traffic safely around the crash. Melissa uses the radio to call an ambulance and a tow truck. She gives first aid to the driver.

Fun Fact:
The United States has more than 12,600 city police departments and 3,070 sheriffs' departments.

12:30 in the
afternoon

What do police officers do when they are not stopping crime?

Police officers help their communities. They want people to be safe and healthy. Today, David and Melissa tell kids about the dangers of drugs. Flash, a police dog, comes along to show how he can sniff out drugs.

Fun Fact:
New Jersey was the first state to have bulletproof vests for all its police dogs.

2:00 in the
afternoon

15

How do police officers know if someone is speeding?

Police officers use radar guns to check vehicle speeds. An alarm on the radar gun sounds. A driver did not slow down for the school zone. David flashes the patrol car's lights. The driver stops. David gives the driver a ticket. He explains that school zones keep kids safe.

What happens at the end of a shift?

Police officers return to the station at the end of their shifts. Officer David returns the patrol car and keys. He fills out reports at his desk. David greets the officers who are coming on duty. It is time for him to go home.

4:00 in the
afternoon

Amazing But True!

The first radios for police cars were made in 1928. The police station could send radio messages to police cars. Officers could only listen. Now police use two-way radios so officers can talk to the station as well.

Equipment Photo Diagram

Lights

Doors
back doors only open from the outside

Cap

Badge

Radio

Gun

Flashlight

Keys

Gloves

21

Glossary

ambulance (AM-byuh-luhnss)—a vehicle that takes sick or hurt people to a hospital

baton (buh-TON)—a small bat officers use to stop criminals from fighting; officers are trained to block punches and knock back criminals safely with their batons.

dispatcher (diss-PACH-ur)—a person who answers 911 calls and assigns rescue workers

patrol (puh-TROLE)—to watch a certain area by walking or riding by it often

radar (RAY-dar)—a machine that uses radio waves to locate objects; police officers use radar guns to measure how fast a vehicle travels.

sergeant (SAR-juhnt)—officer in charge of other patrol officers

shift (SHIFT)—a set amount of time to work

Read More

Englart, Mindi Rose. *Police Officer.* How Do I Become A. San Diego: Blackbirch Press, 2003.

Kottke, Jan. *A Day with Police Officers.* Hard Work. New York: Children's Press, 2000.

Rubinstein, Jonathan. *On the Job with a Police Officer, Protector of the Peace.* On the Job with Bridgit & Hugo. Hauppauge, N.Y.: Barron's, 2001.

Internet Sites

Do you want to find out more about police officers?
Let FactHound, our fact-finding hound dog,
do the research for you!

Here's how:
1. Visit *http://www.facthound.com*
2. Type in the **Book ID** number:
   0736822852
3. Click on **FETCH IT**.

FactHound will fetch Internet sites picked by our editors just for you!

Index